LOVEBIRDS
AS A NEW PET

OLIVER DENTON

CONTENTS

Photos by Dr. Herbert R. Axelrod, H. Bielfeld, Michael De Freitas, Michael Gilroy, Barbara Kotlar, Harry V. Lacey, R. and V. Moat, Horst Muller, Fritz Prenzel, Mervin F. Roberts, T. Tilford, Louise Van der Meid, and Vogelpark Walsrode.

Drawings by Eric Peake, R.A. Vowles.

Distributed in the UNITED STATES by T.F.H. Publications, Inc., One T.F.H. Plaza, Neptune City, NJ 07753; in CANADA to the Pet Trade by H & L Pet Supplies Inc., 27 Kingston Crescent, Kitchener, Ontario N2B 2T6; Rolf C. Hagen Ltd., 3225 Sartelon Street, Montreal 382 Quebec; in CANADA to the Book Trade by Macmillan of Canada (A Division of Canada Publishing Corporation), 164 Commander Boulevard, Agincourt, Ontario M1S 3C7; in ENGLAND by T.F.H. Publications, The Spinney, Parklands, Portsmouth PO7 6AR; in AUSTRALIA AND THE SOUTH PACIFIC by T.F.H. (Australia) Pty. Ltd., Box 149, Brookvale 2100 N.S.W., Australia; in NEW ZEALAND by Ross Haines & Son, Ltd., 82 D Elizabeth Knox Place, Panmure, Auckland, New Zealand; in the PHILIPPINES by Bio-Research, 5 Lippay Street, San Lorenzo Village, Makati, Rizal; in SOUTH AFRICA by Multipet Pty. Ltd., P.O. Box 35347, Northway, 4065, South Africa. Published by T.F.H. Publications, Inc. Manufactured in the United States of America by T.F.H. Publications, Inc.

Introduction

Lovebirds are colorful, playful birds that can make wonderful pets. This is a normal peachfaced lovebird.

Lovebirds are members of the large order of birds known as Psittaciformes—the parrots. They are small little birds ranging in size from 13 cm (5 in) to 16.5 cm (6.5 in). However, their diminutive size belies a very tough nature and the name *lovebird* stems from the way individual pairs will sit very close to each other—not to any willingness to be friendly to other birds. They are native to

Africa and a few offshore islands where they are found, usually in small flocks of 10 to 20 pairs. They are extremely popular birds in aviculture, being hardy, easy to maintain and very willing breeders—in most species. Apart from the "normal" or wild type of lovebirds there are now many color varieties which

The keeping and breeding of lovebirds has become increasingly popular in recent years.

4

have been bred—just as there have been in budgerigars and other birds; indeed, only the budgie has more color varieties available.

In all, there are nine species of lovebird of which eight are available, though certain of these are extremely scarce. Lovebirds are all contained in the scientific genus known as *Agapornis* and are not in any way related to the South American parrotlets you may see in pet stores and which look very similar to them. Of course, parrotlets are also parrots and they look similar to lovebirds because they have developed over thousands of years under conditions similar to those of the

lovebirds. This is known as parallel evolution and is very common in many animal species.

Lovebirds make engaging pet birds and though somewhat more difficult to tame than, say, budgies or cockatiels, you will be rewarded with birds that have lots of character. Readers living in Australia will have a choice of only, at best, four species to choose from; and this is because the export and import of birds to and from that country was banned in January of 1960. Since then two species have been

maintained very well in aviaries while two others, though available, are in very short supply and thus expensive.

In the following text all aspects of keeping these charming parrots will be detailed, together with brief notes on each of the species.

A pair of lovebirds will spend a great deal of time together, usually just watching the activity that is going on around them.

A pair of peachfaced lovebirds, jade green.

Selection

If you are planning on breeding lovebirds then obviously you will purchase one or more pairs of birds, but even if you only want a pet you are still strongly recommended to purchase a pair. The majority of bird species are gregarious and this is certainly true of lovebirds who should never be denied the companionship of their own kind. When you are away from home, they

Always buy the best quality bird you can afford.

will be company for each other and when you are at home they will delight you with their antics.

Obtaining true pairs in most popular species is not easy because the sexes are similar in appearance; when they are different, this is known as being sexually dimorphic. This means that when you see pairs advertised for sale it normally means two birds, not a male and female; in the latter case, the seller will add 'true pair' to the advertisement.

Pet shops will usually stock one or two of the

popular species, such as the peachfaced or Fischer's lovebirds, but should you want the lesser seen varieties or a particular color mutation, then you will need to contact a breeder of these, or one of the specialist bird sellers who advertise in the avicultural press. You may be directed to another potential source of lovebirds if you contact the local bird society. The secretary will no doubt advise you of local members who breed these birds. A visit to a neighborhood cage bird show will also be very productive as you will be able to see the various species, and stock may even be for sale.

I feel that a good class pet shop is deserving of support on the simple grounds that it caters to your bird needs in total, and not just on the faster selling lines. Usually, attendants in pet stores will

Breeders sometimes breed their birds in large groups, called colonies. For the beginner, this would be an overly ambitious venture. It is better to start out in the hobby on a small scale and expand as you acquire the knowledge and skills necessary for successful bird management.

The lovebird you choose should be bright-eyed and alert and should have full plumage. In addition, check the bird's beak and claws for any injuries.

be the owners who will not only have a good knowledge of lovebirds but will take a more personal interest in your being a satisfied customer—after all, they want your repeat seed and accessory business. Do, however, choose those stores that have excellent stock cages which are clean and display only fit birds, not stores where cages are heavily fouled with droppings that have obviously not been removed for many days. Seed should be in containers and not lying around loose in sacks where it can be contaminated. The price of the popular species will be much the same from store to store, so select from a store that has obviously made a good financial investment in its attempt to be as hygienic as possible.

Price

The cost of a pair of lovebirds will be determined

by various factors. Rare species, such as the redfaced, or color mutations, will be more expensive than normal peachfaced, masked or Fischer's lovebirds. A true pair will be higher priced than just a pair (in the sexually non-dimorphic species in particular) and young birds of known age will be priced higher than those of unknown age. Age can be verified if the birds carry closed ring bands on their legs, which are date stamped (of which more is stated under *Breeding*).

Health

A fit, healthy bird is not really difficult to spot, nor is

A masked lovebird. Lovebirds are known for their proclivity to chew on various and sundry items. Keep this in mind when planning your pet's living quarters.

its opposite. The bird should appear active when approached and any that sit huddled in a corner, especially if they are perched on both feet and

In general, lovebirds are hardy, adaptable birds and can be quite content whether housed in a roomy cage or a large aviary.

with their feathers fluffed up, should be avoided. Sometimes an unhealthy bird may be prompted into activity simply by the fright induced by your closeness to the cage, so it is better to stand quietly at a short distance away to see if any birds then settle into this obviously not healthy stance.

The birds for you should have four well-formed toes—two facing forward and two backward, so you can forget any that are deficient or deformed in this aspect. The vent should not be fouled with feces or badly stained as a result of diarrhea. The eyes should be round, open and bright; any signs of weeping indicates ill-health. The cere (just above the beak) and nostrils should be clear of any discharge. The feathers should lay tight against the body and appear immaculate. Sometimes there may be a few feathers missing, but any signs of excessive plucking should alert you to

forget such birds.

Never purchase "cheap" birds unless there is a very good reason for their price which should **not** include "they will molt out to be sound feathered birds next

Any plant materials that your lovebird has access to should be free of pesticides and any other harmful chemical agents.

season." Maybe they will but equally they may be trouble. If required as pets it is essential that you purchase babies straight from the nest; hand-reared will be even better and worth paying the extra cash for them. If you plan to breed then you must purchase young birds; otherwise you risk wasting time trying to breed with birds that are too old or which have proved to have some undesirable aspects to their nature. You can thus see that buying lovebirds is not as simple as it might appear; a bad purchase can ruin your enjoyment of your birds, so do not rush into it. Better still, try and find a friend who has knowledge of lovebirds and who can advise you.

Accommodation

Lovebirds can be kept in aviaries, indoor flights, or cages and they will also breed in each of these types of accommodation. You should prepare the housing before actually going out and buying stock. This applies to even those persons who only want a pair as pets. If you buy the cage at the same time as you buy the birds it will certainly limit your choice to what the one store may have in stock.

For those who plan to have an aviary, caution is the key word where

Opposite: A blue variety of the peachfaced lovebird. As holds true with any kind of pet, you should be fully aware of the responsibilities that come with pet ownership before you purchase any animal.

An indoor flight that has been equipped with a safety porch to prevent the escape of its occupants.

lovebirds are concerned. As a rule of thumb only one pair of lovebirds should be kept per aviary or flight, so if you plan on breeding a number of pairs, then you will need a number of small aviaries, flights or cages—or a mixture of these. If you plan to have a mixed collection of birds in an aviary then be cautious about which species are housed with lovebirds, as

small finches, for example, are at risk of being killed or maimed by these tough little parrots. Even budgies are not safe with most species. You may well see lovebirds living in harmony with other birds—even other lovebirds—but the owners are running a great risk, especially if nest boxes are placed in the aviary as these little birds become even more aggressive in the

Lovebirds are active birds, so it is important that they be provided with adequate exercise space.

If treated with thought and care, lovebirds can thrive in captivitiy.

Aviaries

Lovebirds do not need especially large aviaries and ones with a 2 meter flight (6.5 ft) are adequate. If you have two or more aviaries next to each other, then they should be wired on both sides of the wooden frames; otherwise lovebirds will bite the feet of birds in the adjoining aviary, with possibly very bad injuries being sustained. The essential features of any aviary are that it be made as vermin-proof as possible, and should contain a covered shelter to which the birds can retire at night or during bad weather (frost, cold winds and the like). If the shelter has extra room in it

breeding season. The parents of other species may be bigger and able to look after themselves, but if they have young then these will most likely be attacked by the lovebirds. Bear this aspect in mind when starting up with these otherwise excellent beginners' birds.

Adequate perching space is an important consideration when planning your pet's housing. Your pet shop carries a variety of perches suitable for lovebirds.

in which you can store seed and accessories, then so much the better. There is a vast range of commercially made aviaries on the market and most are advertised in your national avicultural magazine. This is thus a worthwhile weekly or monthly investment to subscribe to, as it will also feature interesting articles on housing, feeding and many other aspects of lovebird management.

Aviary Base

This may be of bare earth, gravel, paving slabs or concrete—the latter three being much easier to keep clean than bare earth. You will not be able to include plants in any parrot aviary, as these would soon be reduced to matchwood by the occupants who have great liking for stripping and/or eating any form of wood. Patches of turf could be placed in a trough and this will give the birds something to peck over and is easily replaced at regular intervals. The perimeter of the aviary floor should have small hole netting placed into the ground to a minimum depth of 31 cm (12 in), and to a similar length at right angles and away from the aviary; this will reduce the chances of mice burrowing into the flight.

Netting

You will need to use weld wire rather than chicken-wire netting as it is both more durable, easier to keep taut and looks better. The size should be 2.5 cm x 1.25 cm (1 x 0.5 in) in order to prevent mice entry (though baby mice can get through this). The gauge to ask for is 19G—though 16G is more suitable, but more expensive. (The gauge is the thickness of the actual wire.) The

A pair of blackcheeked lovebirds. Lovebirds are popular with both beginning and experienced bird keepers.

mesh can be stapled onto a pre-erected frame or can be made into panels which are bolted together, this being more costly but superior in the long run as it can be moved if needed, and is more easily repaired or added to. The frame should be of wood not less than 3.8 cm (1.5 in) thick and this can either be sunk into the earth or be supported on concrete or a wall, in the latter cases being bolted via bolts sunk head first into the concrete or between brickwork and cemented into place.

The Shelter

This can either be a garden shed or similar structure to which the flight has been added or can be built from tongue-and-grooved wood. It should be constructed in such a way as to allow air to circulate and to deny mice a hiding place. Cover the floor with linoleum which is easy to keep clean. Windows, as many as possible, should be covered with mesh so they can be opened during hot weather. The addition of electric light and water will be useful to you. A night light is valuable, as this can be left on (using a low wattage bulb) so that if the birds are startled they do not dash themselves against walls in panic—a common cause of aviary deaths. Ionizers will help keep the air pollution-free. Make sure that electric wiring is out of reach of the lovebirds' beaks! A pop hole will be needed so the birds can go from shelter to flight as required. It will also be useful to have a safety porch on the flight so that the risk of birds escaping as you enter the aviary is thus reduced. A window covered with mesh in the shelter exit door will enable you to see in to the shelter before entering, thus checking if any birds have accidentally escaped the shelter pen area. Perches should be placed at both ends of the aviary and, of course, in the shelter so the lovebirds have somewhere to roost at night. Secure locks should be fitted to all doors as, sad to say, the number of thefts by humans has increased in recent years.

Indoor Flights
These can be built in a spare room, a shed or be part of a large shelter to your aviary. They should be as light and airy (though not drafty) as possible as birds need sunlight to maintain good health. Floors should be such that they are easily cleaned and the walls should be smooth and painted with a washable non-lead-based

Above: Lovebirds are gregarious and will enjoy the companionship of another lovebird.

Opposite: A green pied peachfaced lovebird.

paint. Perches must never be fitted directly over feeding stations and should be placed across the width of the flight so the birds have as much straight flight room as possible.

Indoor flights and cages have the advantage that your lovebirds can be housed in them during hard winters, and will continue to breed throughout such periods if allowed to do so. With indoor situations it is vital that hygiene be of the highest order so that the premises do not become filled with potential diseases.

Cages

These will fall into two basic types. One is the breeder style, which is basically a box structure with a wire cage front, and the other type is the all metal pet cage. The former are available as single, double or triple breeders

and usually have sliding partitions that can be inserted or removed in order to create this variable situation. You will require budgie type fronts, not those used for canaries and other finches. The former have larger doors which open rather than slide up and down. Ideally you want fronts where the wires are horizontal and the supports upright, rather than the reverse; this is because all parrots are fond of clambering up and down such wire fronts. A removable tray should be fitted on the cage floor to facilitate easy cleaning, which should be done daily.

Pet cages should be as large as you can possibly afford—those for budgerigars are suitable but can hardly be described as roomy—the less so if the birds are only infrequently allowed to fly about the room. Your lovebirds will give you much enjoyment and will live for many years, so do give them the most spacious home you can.

Maybe you are a handy person and could build a really large cage into an alcove of your main living room? This can look really smart, or maybe you have room in a conservatory or

The lovebird has attained popularity because of its attractive appearance, lively personality, and comical habits.

patio to erect a meshed-in area that both you and your birds will gain pleasure from. As stated from the outset of this section, give plenty of advance thought to your lovebirds' accommodation and shop around to see what is on the market. Remember, just because it is available does not mean it is good, as cages often seem to be designed by people who have never kept birds and are more concerned with selling you a design concept rather than a practical home for a lovebird. Avoid any that are tall rather than long, as birds need flying space. A good simple oblong or large square is far superior to any with fancy shaped tops which are of no use to the birds themselves.

This bright-eyed lovebird has every appearance of a healthy bird.

Feeding

Variety is the spice of life, so the saying goes, yet it is surprising just how many people do not apply this adage to the feeding of their birds. Lovebirds, like most other parrots, can survive a considerable number of years on a very spartan diet; indeed many are forced to, but this does not make such a diet either satisfying for the bird or good for its long-term well-being. Many

breeding failures can be directly attributed to poor feeding that lacks the variety needed by all birds during the breeding season. Poor feather condition, feather plucking and many ailments are primary or secondary results of an imbalanced diet.

The basic staple diet of lovebirds in the wild is the seeds of various fruits and grasses, but these birds will also eat the fruits themselves, as well as other green food and live food, such as insects. These must

therefore appear in the diet of your stock, and while it would be impossible to equate the wild state foods exactly, what we can do is to ensure that the constituent values of such foods are replaced with others of similar value.

Seed

Differing kinds of seed have different content make-up. Some are rich in carbohydrates, which birds need to provide normal flying and muscular activities, while others are ich in protein, which is needed for bodily growth and tissue replacement. A third group of seeds contains natural fats, and these can be converted by the birds' metabolism into energy carbohydrates or stored as fat which acts as insulation against the cold. Fats also play an important role in helping to absorb vitamins into the body tissues. In the non-breeding season a bird needs seeds rich in carbohydrates but, comes the time for breeding, the lovebirds need extra protein (and many other foods) in order that healthy chicks are produced and reared.

Seeds are deficient of certain vitamins, so these latter items, which are vital for healthy condition, are obtained via green foods. The protein found in seeds is not as readily synthesized by the body as well as is animal protein; thus additional protein via animal tissue is beneficial to all birds. Seeds do not contain all of the minerals needed by a bird and so, again, these are supplied to it via green food. In captivity we can ensure that all vitamins and minerals are supplied to our birds by feeding them with vitamin and mineral supplements which are commercially available at pet shops.

Items such as grit and cuttlefish bone are important sources of essential minerals. Additionally, grit also serves to assist with the digestion of food.

It is important that the seed you buy is of the best quality and has been kept under hygienic conditions. It should not smell moldy nor should it show signs of being fouled by vermin; it must be stored in dry conditions in a jar or metal container (plastic is suitable but tends to cause seed to sweat, which is not good). Cheap seed is usually of poor nutritional value and is very much a case of false economy.

Owners of only two birds will find it pays to purchase either a small parrot mixture, prepackaged, or one of the numerous mixes made up at your local pet store. Breeders will buy larger quantities of the seeds on an individual seed basis, as this is more economic. The preferred seeds are plain canary together with white and panicum millet. This is a typical budgerigar mix and to this can be added white or striped sunflower, hemp, or niger seeds. You do not want obese birds, so feed only high protein seeds prior to and throughout the breeding season, with a few in the colder months of the year. Millet spray will be regarded as a special treat and as such should be fed sparingly.

Green food

You can offer your lovebirds just about any of the greens you would eat, plus wild plants, many of which will be eaten with relish. Avoid picking the latter from areas that may have been treated with chemicals, fouled by dogs or by auto fumes. Carrot tops and the outer green leaves of cabbage species, celery and spinach are all stock favorites of breeders. Try your birds on any fruits such as apple, pear, plums, orange and such, taking note of which they like best. No two birds are quite the same in their feeding habits.

Live food

The range of live food consists of mealworms, maggots, crickets, various flies, and any insects that normally live on green plants. Ant eggs (they are cocoons, not eggs) are another protein-rich form of live food. These can all be purchased from your local pet store or from specialist suppliers who advertise in the avicultural magazines. Pet owners can feed their

Your lovebird can look this healthy if you provide it with a sound diet and if you follow the common-sense rules of good bird management.

birds with one of the supplements rich in protein available from pet stores— though a good balanced seed and green food diet will usually suffice because pet

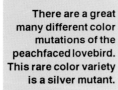

There are a great many different color mutations of the peachfaced lovebird. This rare color variety is a silver mutant.

birds are not as active, and need somewhat less proteins than aviary or breeding stock.

Water

Birds must *always* have access to fresh water, which should be replenished each day. Medicines can often be given via the water supply and also, if a bird is feeling "off color," while it might not eat as much as normal, it will most certainly still drink as much or more than normal.

Grit & Cuttlefish Bone

All parrots husk their seed before swallowing it, but they can crush it only to a limited extent as they have no teeth. The seed is ground into a pulp in their stomach by the muscles of the stomach together with the action of grit which they eat. This can be purchased from your local pet store and has usually been fortified with other needed minerals. Cuttlefish bone is a valuable source of calcium and can be purchased from your supplier and then clipped to the aviary or cage wire. Some can be crushed into a powder and sprinkled onto the seed.

Feeding Pots

Seed can be dispensed via automatic hoppers of various styles or it can be given in pots of earthenware or types which are clipped to the cage wires. The

Perches and branches must be kept clean; they must also be replaced from time to time, as they wear down.

31

disadvantages of hoppers is that they can become blocked at the outlet and need to be tapped regularly to ensure that the seed is falling down as it should. Pots are more easily fouled and will need blowing more often to be sure the husks are removed—otherwise you might think the bird has seed when actually it has a pot full of husks! I prefer to use pots simply because I feed the various seeds separately, this being less wasteful when one has a number of birds. Further, the more "automated" a system becomes the less time one will spend watching the birds to see all is well—but this is purely a personal viewpoint coming from years of habit.

A final point in respect to feeding is that you should always have more than one feeding station in an aviary—especially if it houses numerous birds. This way, the more timid types are not kept away from the seed by aggressive self-assertive types. Aviary birds are best fed in the shelter, where the food is less likely to be fouled by wild bird droppings. It will also encourage the birds into the shelter in the evening.

You can offer your lovebird premixed, packaged seed, or you can make up your own seed mixture. The important thing to remember is that the seeds should be fresh and of good quality.

Lovebird Species

Virtually all birds kept in aviculture are known by two names; one is their common name and the other is their scientific nomenclature. In the case of the former this can vary from place to place even within one country, and of course it varies between differing nations with different languages. The scientific name remains the same regardless of the language. In pet shops the birds will be sold under their common name, but in books, reference articles and zoos, both the common and scientific names will be used. This is because by using the scientific name there can be no possible confusion over what species is being discussed.

The class Aves is divided into many groups and these into further groups, based on similarities between birds, until one arrives at the individual species, which is given two names that, when used together, are unique to that particular species. The first name identifies the group of birds, in this case the lovebirds, and is known as the genus. The second name identifies the species within that genus. Lovebirds are of the genus *Agapornis*

Dutch blue ino peachfaced lovebird.

Nyasa lovebird.

Madagascar lovebird.

which contains nine members—note that the genus and trivial names are normally written in italic, with the genus commencing with a capital letter.

Although eight of the nine species are available to bird keepers, three have become especially popular and the others are now far less frequently seen than in past years. The species that is unknown to aviculture is Swindern's (Black-Collared), *Agapornis swinderniana,* which we thus need not discuss. Of the other eight, three show sexual dimorphism, while four are known as the white eye-ring group. This refers to a bare area of skin around the eyes (none of these four

are dimorphic). The most popular lovebird is undoubtedly the peachfaced, which has now been bred in a number of most attractive color mutations; both the masked and the Fischer's are also popular and both have color mutational forms. Strangely enough, the rarest of the lovebirds, the redfaced, is probably the oldest known species, believed to have been kept as a pet as long ago as the 16th century. This variety was once imported in very large numbers but today it is expensive and you are most unlikely to see it in a pet shop. This also applies to the other remaining four species for which you will need to contact a breeder to acquire,

in most cases.

Sexually Dimorphic Species
Abyssinian Lovebird
(Blackwinged) *Agapornis taranta* Ethiopia. An all green bird with a red beak. The male has a red forehead which the females lack. There is black in the wings. Possibly the hardiest of the lovebirds, these are also, along with the redfaced, the quietest of the group. They are not easy to breed which may account for their loss of popularity compared to former years. Vitamin B is important to these birds, who are more cosmopolitan in their diets than most lovebirds.

Redfaced Lovebird
Agapornis pullaria Guinea, Zaire, Ethiopia, Sudan and Tanzania.

These are dark green birds with a red beak. The chest and neck show suffusions of yellow and the forehead and throat are bright red. Upper rump is blue and underwings black. The face of the hen is more orange, and she lacks the black under her wings. These are the most difficult lovebirds to breed, which is a pity as they are quiet, rather shy and the least aggressive of the genus. They can be colony bred. They nest in termites' nests in the wild (the termites then seal themselves off from the bird's nest) and need comparable nests in which they can tunnel.

Blackcheeked lovebird.

Redfaced lovebird.

Dutch blue peachfaced lovebird.

35

The peachfaced is one of the most commonly known species of lovebird.

Madagascar Lovebird (Grayheaded) *Agapornis cana* Madagascar (Malagasy Republic). The cock is an attractive bird with darker green feathers on the back and wings, and an apple green abdomen. The entire head and chest is a whitish gray; the beak is horn colored. The hen lacks the gray areas and her beak is darker. Until the late 1940s these were quite popular lovebirds but lost ground with the arrival of the Fischer's, Nyasa, and masked—plus the color mutations of the peachfaced. They are now quite rare though occasionally imported. They would make an interesting program for a breeder as no strains of aviary-bred birds are available. Along with the peachfaced they are the most aggressive with both their own kind (conspecifics) and with other birds.

Sexually Similar Species
Peachfaced Lovebird (Rosyfaced) *Agapornis roseicollis* Namibia, Angola, NW Cape Province. The color is a soft mid-green on the back which gets lighter on the underparts. Forehead and face are a pastel rose pink while the rump is blue and tail feather black. The beak is horn colored. These have always been popular birds and their beauty is spoiled only by their rather noisy screeching voice and disposition not incomparable with Attila the Hun! However, this is in mixed company but as pairs they are very affectionate with their mates and can make quite

delightful pets—kept in pairs, remember. They are prolific breeders year 'round and are good parents; they are freely available in Australia, where they are well established.

Fischer's Lovebird
Agapornis fischeri S. Kenya—N. Tanzania. This is a colorful lovebird with a green body, lighter on the under parts contrasting with the deep orange of the face which becomes tinged with almost yellow ochre on the chest and neck. There is blue

A lovely trio of Abyssinian (or blackwinged) lovebirds. The males of this species have red foreheads.

37

in the rump feathers and the beak is orange-red. A few color mutations are available. Like peachfaced, they are not to be trusted in mixed company. They are available in Australia, but

Yellowcollared), *Agapornis personata* NE Tanzania. The masked lovebird is a very striking bird, having dark green feathers on the back and wings, yellow on the chest, abdomen and neck,

scarce though the numbers increase annually as they are good breeders.

Masked Lovebird (Blackmask or

and a black mask covering the head set off by the white eye-ring. They are prolific breeders, bettered only by the peachfaced. In Australia they are popular and reasonably easy to obtain. There are a number of mutation colors available, and in character they are much like other lovebirds—not trustworthy in mixed company. They were first known to aviculture between the two World Wars.

Nyasa Lovebird (Lilian's) *Agapornis lilianae* NW Mozambique— E. Zambia. The Nyasa could easily be mistaken for the Fischer's and a description would read much the same. Like the masked, they first appeared in about 1926

though they were known since 1894. They are the smallest of the lovebirds and have become rather scarce in aviaries, though they are reliable breeders. They can be colony bred, and many have been in Australia, where they are still available in good numbers, though these are receding as the years roll on. They are more sociable in mixed aviaries than other lovebirds, so their drop in popularity is rather surprising.

Blackcheeked Lovebird (Blackfaced) *Agapornis nigrigenis* SW Zambia. These birds are somewhat similar to the Nyasa except that the orange on the face is replaced by brown, which can be so dark as to appear black. They were known to bird keepers from the turn of this century and were very popular. However, the arrival of other species saw the blackcheeked's popularity fall off considerably. Furthermore, many were hybridized with Nyasas so that genuine blackcheeks became even harder to find. Today, the species is an aviary rarity, but those acquiring true pairs will find them very willing breeders.

A silver pied mutant of the peachfaced lovebird.

Breeding

In this small book it is not possible to detail the breeding requirements of all the species of lovebirds, and the subject will be discussed in more general terms.

For some hobbyists, breeding is the most challenging and interesting part of their hobby. If you are interested in breeding lovebirds, it is important that you start with quality stock.

Interested readers who wish to breed a particular species should consult one of the larger volumes on lovebirds, from T.F.H. Publications and widely available in pet shops.

strongly advised not to attempt colony breeding with lovebirds, who have long-standing reputations for being aggressive with other birds and with their own kind, to the point of killing

Some breeders believe that natural pairing is the best way to obtain a good pair of birds.

Breeding Systems

Lovebirds can be bred either in groups, which is called colony breeding, or in pairs which are housed in their own aviaries or breeder cages. Beginners are

other pairs and/or the chicks of these. Colony breeding is successfully undertaken by experienced aviculturists but is a specialized area best left until one has kept various species.

Obtaining a True Pair

Because the popular lovebirds are all sexually similar, obtaining a true breeding pair can be difficult. Surgical sexing and feces analysis can be undertaken these days but is expensive. Other methods are far less reliable, so you are advised to pay a little extra and purchase a known true pair from a breeder; pet shops rarely have guaranteed pairs for sale. This will save you a lot of time and possible wasted effort and will be cheaper in the long run.

Breeding Condition

You must not attempt to breed with birds that are not in hard, fit condition. They should not be overweight—especially the hen,or she will probably become egg-bound. It is important that prior to the breeding period the pairs are given plenty of aviary exercise or indoor flight room. An unfit cock may result in unfertilized eggs. These are termed clear eggs. In the weeks prior to breeding, the diet of the birds should start to include more protein seeds, live food, extra calcium (such as

A group of peachfaced lovebirds. It is exciting and rewarding to see your baby lovebirds grow up into beautiful adults such as these.

bread soaked in milk), and extra vitamins via green food or supplements. This diet must be maintained throughout the breeding period; it will peak during the first few weeks of the chicks' lives when the hen needs to feed them often—and retain her own strength.

Nest boxes

One of the problems with lovebirds is that they roost in their nest boxes. This means they will invariably breed throughout the year, including the winter months when you do not want them to. This can be overcome by removing them to indoor flights or cages or, sometimes, by not giving them nesting material and removing it from their nests.

Nest boxes are best situated under a covered part of the aviary, and if breeding is in cages, fit the nest box on the outside so that nest inspection is possible without undue problems. The type of nest boxes favored by lovebirds are larger budgerigar types or grandfather clock ones. Lovebirds require much nesting material in the form of fresh twigs, grasses and moss as they tend to continue adding to the nests even after the clutch of eggs is laid. However, an overlarge box is not needed as most birds prefer the security of a snug fit for themselves. The hen incubates the eggs and feeds the chicks while they are in the nest; the cock will roost with her overnight. Species such as the redfaced require specialized nest boxes so they can build a small tunnel in them.

Eggs

The clutch size can vary

These baby lovebirds will be completely independent by the time they are six to eight weeks old.

feeding routine.

Rearing Chicks

Once the youngsters are old enough to feed themselves, they should be removed from the

from one to eight eggs with three to five being normal. These are incubated in 21–24 days and fledging takes between 38–45 days, during which the cock takes an increasing share of the

parents, who might otherwise attack them—especially if the hen has commenced laying a second round of eggs. They should continue to receive a wide diet from you and seed

should be placed both in pots and on the floor of their stock cage until they are accustomed to feeder pots or hoppers.

Identification

Chicks can have metal or plastic rings placed on their legs when they are a few days old. When ordering these from a pet shop or bird society, state the species. Closed rings are needed for

lovebirds as they can easily remove split rings. Those which are dated will provide a record of age. Have an experienced breeder show you how to place the rings on and, once fitted, always keep an eye on them so they never become too tight or clogged with debris.

Egg binding

Hens can become egg-bound if they are overweight or if their diet is lacking in essential vitamins or minerals. They are

Lovebirds are a good choice for the beginning breeder.

Group of redfaced lovebirds pictured at 30 days of age.

47

unable to pass an egg and unless this is freed they will likely die. Place a hen who appears to be struggling into a warm cage—ideally a hospital cage where a temperature of 30°C (85°F) can be maintained. If this fails, then call your veterinarian urgently and he will remove the egg surgically—do not attempt this yourself. Once clear of the egg, the hen should be

"If for any reason you have a need to foster eggs or chicks, they can be placed under any hen of comparable breeding state, that is, who has eggs of the same age."

ept in a warm room and not
eturned for breeding until
he is fully fit.

ostering

If for any reason you have
need to foster eggs or
chicks, they can be placed
under any hen of comparable
breeding state, that is, who
has eggs of the same age. It
is not unknown for
budgerigars to foster
lovebirds.

As a general rule,
nestboxes should be
relatively small and
compact. A perch
located just below the
entrance will give the
lovebirds easy
access to the nesting
site.

Health Problems

Many ailments that lovebirds suffer can be attributed to either poor management routine or an unbalanced diet. Prevention is therefore better than cure. There are many areas of husbandry that can easily be overlooked because one is always short of time, and from these minor problems, major ones may develop.

Overcrowding and Stress

Although you may keep your lovebirds in pairs, you may be tempted to put too many cages into too small an area—or you may reduce the size of the cages. This increases the risk of airborne viruses. Ionizers help combat

his, and cleanliness is most important. Keeping in too small a cage will increase the risk of stress. This will mean your bird's resistance to illness reduces, so minor ailments can become major problems. Incompatible pairs will mean one bird is continually stressed (usually the male in lovebirds) and more prone to illness.

Quarantine

When you acquire additional stock, ideally it should be kept well away from the rest of your collection for at least ten days—this will allow any illness it is carrying to show itself. If this is not done, and if the bird is incubating an illness, it will quickly spread to other birds.

Cleaning

Always wash your hands after handling each bird. This can become a real chore but it is an extra safeguard. Have spare stock cages so that when one is vacated it can be scrubbed with a mild disinfectant and left empty for a week or more. Do not keep perches overlong— replace them on a regular basis. Cracked feeder pots or hoppers should be discarded; they harbor germs. A spare aviary is always preferred, as you can periodically move stock so that one can be left empty for a month or two (after it has been thoroughly cleaned and perches replaced). Nest boxes in particular can harbor red

With careful attention, your lovebird can remain in good health for many years.

Sometimes illness is brought into an aviary by a new bird. Even if you have purchased a lovebird from a reputable dealer or breeder, a quarantine period is strongly recommended.

Opposite: Overgrown claws should be clipped. Great care must be taken, however, that the blood vessel which runs through part of each claw is not cut.

mites. These suck the blood of adults and chicks during the night and then hide in crevices during the day. Heavy infestations can build up and cause havoc, even death, in your birds. Always have ample spare boxes so you can dismantle and disinfect the nest boxes on a rotational basis. Red mites are easily treated with proprietary medications, but they should never have become a problem in the first place.

Nutrition

A poor diet that lacks essential vitamins, minerals or proteins will mean your bird's resistance to disease is always at a low level, and it quickly succumbs to ailments it would normally have no problem with. Lovebirds need plenty of bark, such as apple, pear or other fruit branches, to chew. Be sure, of course, that the branches have come from trees which have **not** been sprayed with insecticide of any kind. This provides them with certain ingredients but also keeps them busy thus reducing the risk that they will become feather pluckers (their own or their mates') out of boredom.

Diarrhea

Unduly copious or green feces indicate something amiss; if combined with general lethargy, running nose or eyes then

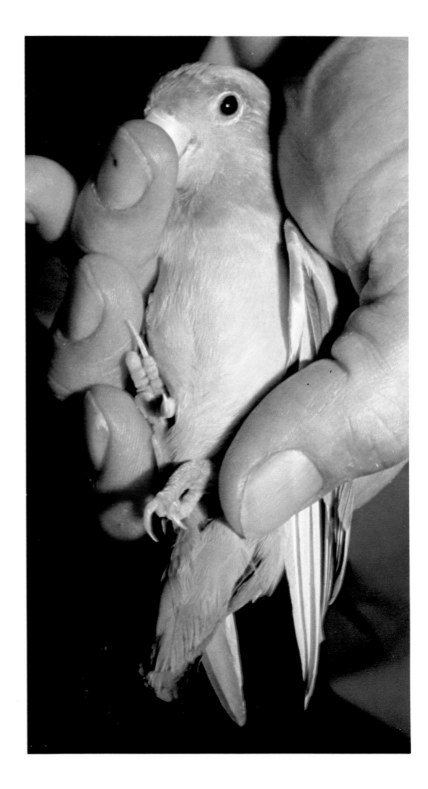

it can be symptomatic of many conditions. The best course is to isolate the bird(s) immediately and place it (them) in a warm environment with constant temperature being maintained. Call your veterinarian, as it may be a major illness about to be spread right through your stock. It may only be a

minor problem, but the vet can advise and take feces for examination.

Parasites

Many problems stem from various external and internal parasites in the form of worms or lice. Worms can be ingested when food that has been fouled by wild bird droppings is eaten. Your vet can supply suitable treatments and you are advised to worm your pairs before breeding to reduce the risk of these parasites being passed via the hen to the chicks.

Exposure to disease, a drop in temperature, malnutrition or any other stressful situation can endanger the health of your lovebird.

Pet Lovebirds

The comments made in respect to feeding and general care are every bit as applicable to a pair of pet lovebirds as to a complete stud of these parrots. Usually, pet birds are less prone to illness than are aviary birds because they are not exposed to quite the same risks. However, there are other considerations to be allowed for. It is important that your bird's cage is situated in a draft-free position—preferably against a wall, as this will give it security on that side. The bird should be able to benefit from direct sunlight but must **never** be placed where it cannot escape the sun's rays when it wishes. In centrally heated homes where there may be a wide fluctuation between day and night-time temperatures, your pet may well appear in a constant state of molt. This is not ideal, though pets appear to adjust to this situation; even so, try to maintain as near to constant temperatures as you can. In order to keep its feathers in excellent condition you should spray your lovebird with tepid water at least once per

week—and the provision of a bird bath may or may not be used by the lovebirds. They will enjoy a spray once they are accustomed to it.

Pets should be given as much free-flying time in your room as possible but ensure that potential hazards are removed and exits closed. Electric wires, cats, aquariums without hoods, open fires, and open vents are all hazards that must be considered. A bird restricted to a cage all its life is a sorry animal and should this become its lot, then do it a favor and find it a new home. The more time you can spend with your pets the more pleasure you will receive from them and the tamer they will become. If you purchased a lovebird straight from the nest, then it will soon become finger-tame, but if it is an older

bird, then it will require considerable patience to arrive at this state.

A striking lutino peachfaced lovebird. No matter what species of lovebird you choose, you will grow to love your lovebird for his amusing and endearing behavior.

I strongly advise readers to purchase only baby lovebirds for pets, because otherwise you may give up on trying to tame them and thus they will become purely "inmates" of their cage. Lovebirds have been known to learn to

Opposite: Lovebirds are alert, inquisitive birds that will enjoy exploring their surroundings.

peak a few words but never count on this as the chances are very slim indeed and the birds would need many, many hours devoted to them. If it happens, great, but it is their personalities that is their main charm.

Mutational Colors

It has been mentioned that certain species have mutant colors, and some of these are especially attractive. Lutinos (yellow) always stand out—here the green is replaced by yellow. There are lutino peachfaced, masked, Fischer's and

Nyasas of varying shades. The blue-masked lovebird is very striking with the green replaced by a wonderful shade of blue. There are many other mutational colors, but these are not always as attractive as they sound; but it will certainly pay you to visit a breeder who has numerous of these, though the normal wild colors always take some beating.

Index

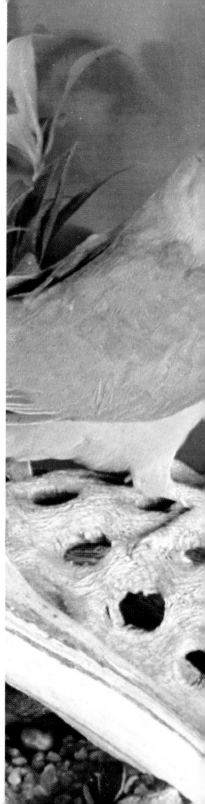